—Read, read, read!
Best Wishes,
John Bil

Oh, How I Wished I Could Read!

Written By John Gile • Illustrated by Frank Fiorello

10   9   8   7   6   5   4   3   2

Library of Congress Card Number: 94-096745
Library Reinforced ISBN: 0-910941-10-6
Paperback ISBN: 0-910941-11-4

Printed in the United States of America
by Worzalla, Stevens Point, Wisconsin

To The People Who Give Help And Hope, Especially
Jean, Nick, Glenn, Mimi, Ruth, Al, Margaret, Joe, Toni,
Andrea, Mark, Brian, Sue, Claude, Bob, Renie, ABCDEFSM,
And To The Precious Little Ones Who Call Me Grandpa.

J.G.

To My Wife Susan
And Our Daughters Cara And Lisa
With Love And Laughter.

F.F.

I awoke with a yell
and sat straight up in bed,
full of fear and wild worries
and trouble and dread.

Was it just a bad dream?
Or was what I feared true?
Was reading a feat
only others could do?

In my dream,
I was walking
alone on the street

And decided to sit down and put up my feet.

I discovered
too late
what the
"Wet Paint" sign said
when the bench
left my back side
a bright shade of red.

Then I saw
a cute puppy
and wanted
to pet it.

A sign tried to warn me I'd better forget it.

But the words on the gate
meant nothing to me

I ill a pack of wild dogs chased me right up a tree.

I continued along on my readingless way, having no way to know what each sign had to say.

I wished I could read
'cause then I could know
when danger signs warned me
where I shouldn't go.

A sign said, "No Crossing," but I didn't heed it because, in my dream, I had no way to read it.

So I stepped off the sidewalk and, oh, what a fuss: I was nearly run down by two cars and a bus!

I heard honking and beeping, tires squealing and shrieking, cars crashing and smashing and scraping and screeching.

The drivers were angry. One yelled, all agreed: "What's the matter with you? You should learn how to READ!"

I jumped from the street and ran away **fast,**

ut
worried
about each
sign that
I passed.

A bove and beside and behind and below
were instructions and warnings I needed to know.

In my
readingless dream,
I felt angry and sad,
as if I had lost
a best friend
— and I had.

 was lost and alone and afraid as could be
of the readingless troubles still waiting for me.

 wandered and wondered what words I saw meant,

Then got stuck
in the muck
near a sign —
"Wet Cement."

So I took off my shoes and sat down to clean them.

wo signs blocked my way,
    but I sat down between them.

They said, "Poison Ivy," but I didn't know

When I headed for home to get medication, I went from a bad to a worse situation.

 opened
the cupboard
to look
for toe
ointment,

But all that I found
there was more
disappointment.

Each bottle and tube on the shelf had a label
I needed to read, but I wasn't able.

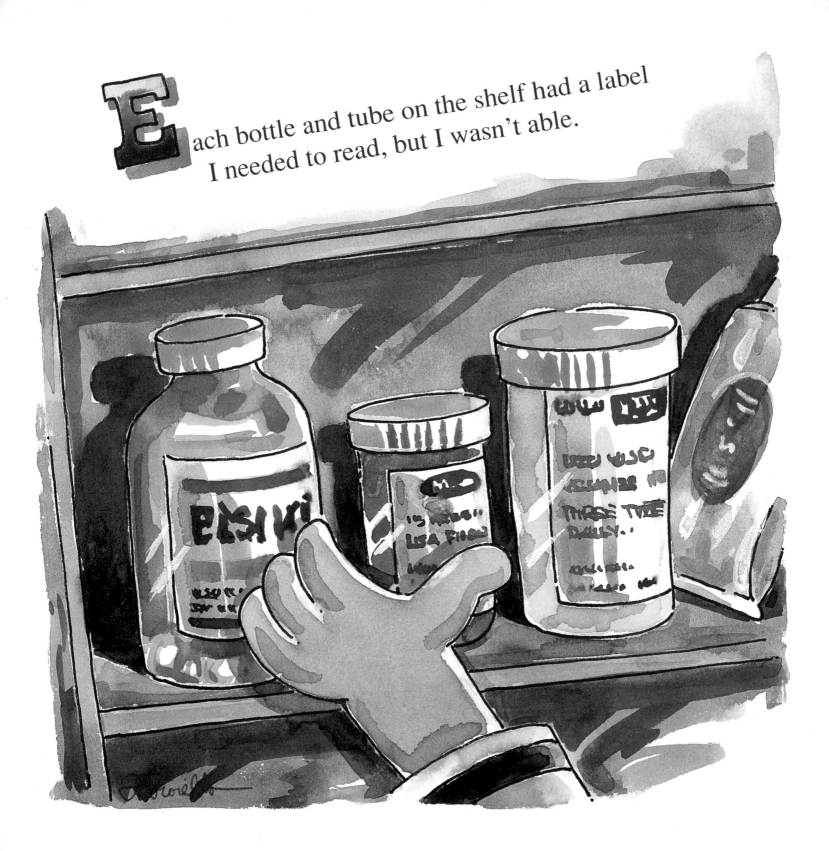

 itched
and
I
twitched.
How I
wished I
could
READ!

My toe was on fire from that poisonous weed.

Just then I woke up
from my
readingless dream
when my cat
nipped my toe
and I let out a scream.

OUCH >

threw back my covers
and jumped to the floor.

I ran to the shelf
  where my books were before.

Could I tell a "b"
from a "t" or a "z"?
Or were letters just lines on the paper to me?

My books told the story,
   as storybooks do:
My dream was a nightmare,
   completely untrue.

I can read

If you wonder in winter

At last it was over!   *At last I was freed*

From the night when I wished, how I wished I could read!